THE GREAT WORLD OF DAYS

*a collection of poetry published
in Bourgeon 2007-2021*

EDITED BY GREGORY LUCE,
ANNE BECKER, AND JEFFREY BANKS

Book design by Shannon Pallatta
Cover art © Pat Goslee

Editor Bios

Gregory Luce is the author of *Signs of Small Grace, Drinking Weather, Memory and Desire, Tile*, and *Riffs & Improvisations*. He was the 2014 Larry Neal Award winner, awarded by the DC Commission on the Arts and Humanities. He writes a monthly column on the arts for Scene4 magazine. He is retired from National Geographic, works as a volunteer writing tutor/mentor for 826DC, and lives in Arlington, VA.

Anne Becker is author of *Human Animal, The Transmutation Notebooks: Poems in the Voices of Charles and Emma Darwin*, and *The Good Body*. Also a teacher, she works with poets putting together chapbooks and full length collections and was senior producer of Watershed Tapes, recording series of acclaimed poets reading their work. Now a paper artist, she prints her poems on paper that she has made.

Jeffrey Banks is poetically known as "Big Homey". His credits include Essence Magazine, Sirius/XM Satellite Radio, Radio-One Inc., the CBS Early Show, and Black Enterprise Magazine. He has performed nationwide, on international broadcasts, and is recipient of multiple awards and publications through DC Public Libraries, the National Association for Poetry Therapy, Paris Lit Up and Day Eight.

Advance praise for *The Great World of Days*

"I am continually amazed at the excellent poetry Day Eight has produced; and now we have The Best of The Best in *The Great World of Days*—poems compiled from poets who have passed through the Bourgeon portal. Every human story is here—the wry, the sorrowful, the wondrous, the exalted, the humorous. I have not read better poetry anywhere; and if you have this anthology, you'll have everything you need for each season of your life. You can keep it at your bedside and always find something new to love."

Grace Cavalieri
Maryland Poet Laureate

"Here reside the voices of the DMV (DC/MD/VA) in an anthology with a breadth expanding wider than the Potomac River. A work representative of the heart and pulse of the tristate area through sight, sounds, and memories. Each piece gives a glance into a space in time, an event, a love, an idea, a concept, desire, or even trauma. These stories create a beautiful tapestry illustrating the beauty of our creative collective."

Monica Leak, M.Div., M.L.S., M.A.CCC-SLP
Author of *For Her Name's Sake*

"This is a collection of colors, a prism of poems. A bright, dark, sunshine-midnight of words. Offered by many fine poets, the work within The Great World of Days kaleidoscopes emotions, from introspection, anger, wonder and delight to reminiscence, lament and whim. The time a reader spends alongside such shimmers will be time counted towards Yes!"

Hiram Larew
Author of *Mud Ajar*

"The Bourgeon Anthology weaves together some of the most undeniably unique poets of Washington D.C.'s diverse artistic community, and thus the world. Dense with surrealist voices from inside hospitals, blazing houses, and modern paintings, to the opulent goddess with cinematic tales of omnipotent nameless ancestors effortlessly illustrating iridescent land-scapes. Every luminous lament, dialogue and inner voice found in this anthology serves as serene observations into nature's elements beyond metaphors and sensational imagery, there is humour too. From haikus to confessionals, sonnets to original descriptive experimental forms, these inspiring poems live beyond the page, stage or any caged mind that misinterprets them. Through the Bourgeon Anthology, there is a vital con-temporization of the necessity to challenge what it means to see, be seen, and share a vision of the unseen resilient nature of truth-telling. Bottom line, this is the most inspiring anthology I've read this year because it speaks to every aspect of every global contemporary experience externally and internally, socially, spiritually and psychologically. For any reader with intellectual insomnia, this anthology will settle your restless anxiety simply by proving to you that there are at least 81 pages of other minds just like yours searching and sharing."

Malik Crumpler
Paris Lit Up

"Truth and story-telling link limbs, moving the fingers and toes of wideawake—woke— poems by many Washington DC area poets in *The Great World of Days.* Forget reservations, walk in, grab hold for better transportation."

Karren LaLonde Alenier
Author of *how we hold on*

"Washington DC is best known as the place that hosts Power with a capital P. But, it's something else too, something very different—a city with a distinguished and vibrant culture all its own. That culture has been created by the exceptionally diverse mix of people who have deep roots here, & also by the many people who come here from around the world—and come to stay. Bourgeon, a magazine published by the non-profit arts organization Day Eight since 2005, has introduced a wealth of critical and creative work by visual and performance artists as well as writers, most of whom call the District of Columbia home. The poems here have been selected from among hundreds published in the magazine from 2007-2021. In a place where the local news is often world news, the poets brought together in these pages find the familiar and the extraordinary in everyday lives, in histories and experience worth consideration. *The Great World of Days* offers their views of neighborhoods, families, immigrants, busboys, jazz clubs, birds and trees, and themes of love and hate, illness and loss, patriotism and resistance. Movie-maker John Waters makes an appearance, and the mysterious "Throne of the Third Heaven of the Nations Millennium General Assembly," an obscure masterpiece beloved by many Washingtonians, is honored in a poem of its own. Curious? Come inside and see."

Beth Baruch Joselow
Author of *Excontemporary*

"*The Great World of Days* gathers a remarkable breadth of American voices in poems that range from the reflective to the plaintive, the mournful, the angry, and the polemical. In lyrical narratives, homages, elegies, and responses to art, the poets here give us unique verbal lenses into their mindful preoccupations."

Merrill Leffler
Author of *Mark the Music*

"The Story of My Father" by Holly Karapetkova originally appeared in Harpur Palate and also in Towline (Cloudbank Books, 2016)

"Patriotism Reconsidered" by Lucinda Marshall originally published in the Transition Poem series by Indolent Books. It was one of a series of poems read at the Arlington Writers Resist event January 15, 2017.

"Driving to Juniata" by Katherine Young was first published in qarrtsiluni. It was first in a series of poems read at the Arlington Writers Resist event January 15, 2017

"The Beginning of Prayer" by Sarah Katz was first published as a postcard as 2015 winner of the District Lit Poetry Prize

"Working Farm for Sale" by J.D. Smith was first published in Think Journal

Foreword

This anthology collects the best poems from approximately 14 years of poetry offered by Bourgeon.

Bourgeon, the journal published by Day Eight, was originally founded to provide a forum for working artists to present and discuss their work through artist-authored features about exhibits and performances in and around the Washington, D.C., area. Since the first printed issue, the journal also published original poems by local poets. Some time before I joined the Board of Day Eight I took on the role of Literary Editor for Bourgeon, succeeding Jessica Wilde. We began actively soliciting work, first from D.C.-area poets and later from those elsewhere. We published then as we still do on a rolling basis.

In 2020 we launched a new mechanism for online submissions which has attracted poets from all over and contributed to the ongoing professionalization of our poetry publishing. This book contains work from 54 poets, most residing locally (or who did at the time their poems were published), with a few from around the country. The dates of publication range from 2007 to early in 2021. We are proud of the diversity of voices, ages, styles and themes and the quality of all the work presented. Rather than highlight individual poems/poets as is sometimes customary, I invite the reader to browse the pages and find poems that speak or sing to her and perhaps discover some work that moves him in unexpected ways.

Our efforts to present and support poets and poetry continue to grow as this book goes to press. In 2017, Day Eight launched the DC Poet Project, a search for poets in our region who do not have access to traditional means of publishing. The four winners to date have all produced splendid books and as of this writing we anticipate another fine volume as the 2021 series concludes.

Even as this volume celebrates the poetry first published in Bourgeon, we are working on transitioning Bourgeon's poetry publishing into its own journal, which will allow us to publish more poems and truly expand our scope to the national and even international level. I undertake that work with the co-editors of this volume, Anne Becker and Jeffrey Banks, who joined me as literary editors of Bourgeon in 2020.

It has been a joy and an honor to have been involved in Day Eight's poetic endeavors this past group of years and I look forward to many more years discovering and promoting the best of local and national poetry. Please enjoy some of the fruits of our labors so far.

Gregory Luce
Board Chair Day Eight and Literary Editor Bourgeon

Table of Contents

The Great World of Days

LAURA MCCARTY

The Home We Will Remember

I am born in the black hills of eastern Kentucky
to a young woman from the Gulf Coast of Texas
who sews matching dresses for her three daughters
and sings at church to the kind of God that requires
service Sunday, Monday, Tuesday, Wednesday,
Thursday, Friday, and the occasional Saturday.
She weeds clover out from under her
orange blossoms, watches her pregnant neighbor
eat paint chips from her window sill
and listens to Rachmaninoff. Appalachia's blue ash
and accordions are not my mother
who grew up picking cotton, a penny a pound.
She begs my father to leave. He doesn't.
For a while. In a tan VW bug
with a diaper pail swishing in the back,
ammonia wafting, my mother drives us away
from the Ashland hills to the home
we will remember, where alligators live
in the swamp near the public swimming pool,
the garbage truck will save us from a four-foot flood,
and my sister will collect tarantulas with broken legs.
We will hide in bathtubs from tornadoes
and water our house in droughts
to keep from losing the foundation.
My sisters and I were birthed in the hollers
but our bodies know
the salt marshes, big sky, and green lizards.
We belong to our mother's land,
its tortillas and fried catfish,
its beaches and its air.

Criminally Black

The preface of my purgatory bore me black and stacked all the
odds against me
No jury to await an impending judgment
Because my complexion already rendered me guilty
Sentenced to death by legalized hate crimes
Metaphorical lynchings of those criminally black in white
America
The land of the free ain't so free for a black man in white
America
Concentration camps didn't begin in Germany
They took their blueprint from white America trying to cancel
out this black album and
Without a reasonable doubt they now use our penal system
Systematic injustices
To implement our slavery
And as successors to our lineage
We're all guilty as American gangsters
And they have unfinished business with the dynasty
Black people:
America promises nothing
40 acres and a mule
And we've yet to receive
Nothing
Have Medgar Evers and Rodney King taught us nothing?
Emmett Till's murderers got away scot-free
Time served was absolutely nothing
But yet Michael Vick does a two-year stint
Because in comparison to a pit
Black life is worth
Absolutely nothing

We are the hunted
Endangered species in this wild jungle we call our home
But we're not even welcome here
We're not even wanted but
If my skin were lighter maybe I'd understand why Dorothy
clicked her heels
And said
There's no place like home
Dethrone the idea that we're on equal playing fields
No this is a slaughter
But it's somehow legal
To take the life of skin darker
So we can't exactly call them robbers
They're monsters of this
Judicial gang called America
And being black is the treason
Killing niggaz back to back it's open season
When being black is a crime
Punishments are acts of
Stand your ground murders
Or enslavements by extensive stints of jail time
So if you ever find yourself seventeen with Arizona Tea
A tall being in a hoodie with skittles
Just don't be black
Because history has taught us
It's that which makes us
Criminal

I Want Better

I want better.
I find this double mindedness debilitating
And I am hating the outcomes that I see
I want to flee from reality
Because of the way the world treats me
You see
I want better.
Seeking my significance in others
Is not what the lover of my soul had in mind
He wants me to find the divine love
And he gives me enough to snuff out
Any enemy
So I would not have to plea
For anyone to validate me
I want better.
I deserve way more than mediocre
And I'm tired of being broker
Than any two cent share
On the stock exchange
I want to proclaim prosperity
Not to brag on myself
But to declare your wealth
So others may know about
Your greatness.
I want better.
I'm mad at me
For allowing the tragedy of people-pleasing
Because of teasing
Lord, you have my best interest at heart and
You want to impart the wisdom of what is coming

I just have to quiet my spirit
So I can hear it.
I want better.
I want the best but sometimes I settle for less
Because silently I felt I was cursed
To be the worst
But in the midst of low self esteem
I still believed in me
And with the vision
Although others may not agree
You said
To wait on me,
Because it will tarry.
I want better.
I plan to see the promised land
But even as the quicksand
Tries to suck me up
Lord you fill my cup
And when I want to doubt God
You work it out
And when life seems barren
You are still caring
And you are daring me to trust you
And that is what I must do if
I want better.

The Thing about Mornings

I'll never forget
We slept
Splayed on memorial benches
Morning dew falling on locks like overgrown caterpillars
Crawling to crystallized captivity
Your smile
Sunrise evaporating what moisture remains
I won't always remember the night
But tucked in the grey folds
Your hips play crescent hillsides
The sun peeking from behind your lips
There is something unforgettably mystic about you
This
A marvel as baffling as frost flying through a cloudless Sunday
brunch
As timeless as each second spent in your presence
As infinite as the space between
For every coat of dew fallen on a night forgotten
There is a cherished morning
Cleaning cobwebs and evaporating what moisture remains.

Annie

I. Lament for Annie
The pink door on Locust street
sits slightly ajar.
Once grand,
now suffering at the hands of too many strangers
who have no idea where they are going.
The vine covered church across the way
still casts an afternoon shadow on the sidewalk
as if nothing has changed,
yet twenty years and you are gone.
Am I the only one who knows
that there has been a disappearance?
A vanishing?
Am I the only one who remembers
what was behind the pink door:
Two rooms on the third floor
filled with the secrets and dreams
of a fragile black girl.
A girl with a distant smile
that never seemed anchored
in anything I could truly understand.
A soul longing to exist in some other place.
There are days when I take Locust street
just to stand in the church courtyard across the way,
searching for a time
that has fallen through the looking glass.
Watching as people walk through my memories of you
carrying away chips of pink paint
on the bottom of their shoes.
Oh Annie,

that door is always open
waiting
for
you.

II. Annie Speaks
Pink is no color for a door
that must withstand
the harshest elements,
the unseeing eye, the unfeeling hand.
How well I know this frailty,
having always craved the rarest tenderness,
the unattainable heart.
Imagine the pale, pale rose
near translucent with innocence,
too delicate for touch.
Have twenty years flown by so wingedly?
Here within the shadow of this hallowed place
time is nothingness. I am everywhere.
My secrets ride aside the wind.
My dreams ascend the vines toward
heaven.
Come. Walk with me across the courtyard
and know that I am home.

Lepidoptera

On a pin, in a box, in a drawer, in a cabinet, in a dusty annex, there it is, your smile, the one upturned on both sides in symmetrical pleasure.

A long-ago clerk handsomely quilled its number, 34, or 558, or whatever, and here today it sits, a lonely representative of its continent of gone-tomorrow wonders. Immortality is a lot to ask of a couple of square inches of pretty iridescence.

If we gave our specimen a sky and a sun again, would it lift from its disenchanted inventory and join all its fellow wings who light momentarily on puddles and brilliant perfect things and then are never seen again?

What are you saving it for? Let us try.

The Bridge of Your Nose is Worth Crossing

The internet is said to house trolls.
With ugly weeping warts and their own URLs,
whatever those are.

I much prefer incarceration.
The way they replace the name I always forget
with a number I can't remember.

That dumb steel clank of the bars dancing together.
Guilty in absentia.

Kafka is my favourite prisoner
because he confesses nothing to everyone.

You find that you keep reading,
offering outs to the author who never
takes them.

The bridge of your nose is worth crossing.
Traffic on either side and a half dozen Rubicons.

It's pine needle gin and race records.
Derailment east of the Rockies.

That selfish clingy way she cries into your shoulder
as though her sadness will be there forever.

A single flicker of candlelight.
Tiny bags of almonds handed out
along the flightpath.

An army of mousetraps in the dark,
so you have to be careful.

On your way to the bathroom
and damn near anywhere else worth
travelling to.

Without a valid passport.
That open ocean way I step into the shower
and take on water.

Build a Brother

Dear Brother,

I have not seen you in fifteen years.
I'm not sure how to miss you.
At first it was easy,
plug in your Super Nintendo
and sit down with a book –
our mutual way of hiding.
Lately it has been accidental,
like when our nephew Sean
played with your Legos.
You always made space ships,
I always made houses.
Sean has never heard your voice,
and I don't know if he ever will.

I pulled your white plastic megaphone
out from a box, my last visit home;
hung it on a hook in the basement.
The metal lip amplified your voice,
reaching further than your arm.
Your voice became grit, pushed against the hallways.
Nothing worked to tame you,
not hearing the version I remembered –
Mom left Dad with both of us.
I remember the loaded station wagon.
You said you believed me, Mom fought for you.
I knew you did not want to live with Dad.
The dry echo of your voice lasted a year.

A Kept Man

If I were yours to keep,
you'd have me in a
gilded case, with a large
brass key dangling gingerly
from your belt loop.
But I am miles
out of touch with you,
in the land of bones and ashes,
and the lid of your case is
chastened with dust;
scarred by passing time
and by disuse.
Am I free?
Does your mind
still roam to me?
My heart pleads to you, "Find me!
I lie amid the ruins
of an epoch
that may yet exist.
Return!"
By what light shall I search
but by the glint of sunbeam
off a small, brass key.
Do you still carry
such a candle?
Oh, let it be so!

Broken

I dropped my glasses by mistake
I was certain that they shattered

The right lens was intact
The left lens, had become detached

Separate, but unbroken
With little to no effort
I was able to put it back in its proper place

What if every time we thought we were broken
We were really just taking a break

From being entirely whole

Don't Take Advice From Strangers

With thanks to Natalie Shapiro's "Sunshower"

Some people say you can't feel color.
They say touch doesn't have a sound.
They say breathing is not
the same thing as listening,
that you can't pull love, beating,
out of you, can't hold it hot and throbbing
in your palms, can't hurl it across a room,
can't make it stop singing.
Some people say you can hear
a whisper from yards away
but only if you stand on a rock
placed equidistant from another rock
outside of a building that arcs
like a moving train.
Some people say the words
will not hurt when they hit you.
Hold still: Here is a blue to cut your teeth on,
a heaviness on the tongue,
a buzzing at your lips, a noise like silence,
a space like a body,
a murmur like bees inside your ears.

What You Left Behind

A closet full of tools
I cannot name.
An industrial-strength vacuum.
Receipts from 2005.
Books you never read.

A 40-foot ladder.
Empty, crusted paint cans.

Years of dust in the corners
we never swept.
Cracked windowsills and peeling paint.
Curtains hung crookedly.
Others never hung.

The bed we bought together.
And the sheets we slept on.
How many years.

Dreams where I sense you
lying next to me
and wake up
saying no, no, no.

Your last name
on every document I own.
The hollow of its vowels.

MARIANNE SZLYK

Fishing Poem

The grandfather I never knew fished for hornpout
in a pond I heard about but never saw.

There my mother's family spent summers,
less than a half-hour's drive from the city.

Unless they fished in clear water,
hornpout tastes like mud, which not even

Gram's hand-cranked peach ice cream
or Grandpa's Lucky Strike Greens could disguise.

I Google Ashburnham to see the pond
not quite sparkle under a brilliant sky.

The surface hides mud, weeds, a murder victim.
No one fishes now, and the houses for sale

are far grander than that summer-time shack
without electricity, without running water.

The trees are smaller than they would have been
before the hurricane, the year my mother turned twelve,

the year she stopped fishing.

Factually

facts
are
stones:
quiet,
unchangeable
context.

if you turn
a stone
in your hand,
it presents
different aspects
of itself.

if you look
at the fifteen stones
in the garden of
Ryōan-ji, you will see
only fourteen, no matter
where you stand.

if you submerge
a stone, its color
will intensify,
even transform,
without changing
the fact of stone.

if you suppress
stone, pressurize

a molten fact,
it will erupt
in unanticipated ways.

if you holler
in a canyon, stone
will reverberate with echoes.

stone is more ancient than words,
as deep as bedrock, oceanic crust, iron core
as broad as spinning planets circling a universe of stars.
like truth, like love, a fact is the pebble in your shoe, the jewel
in your palm.

The Busboy

(Juan Romero, 1951-2018)

Fifty years gone, I still can't sleep.

When I took up that platter
of sandwiches to his room,
the Senator greeted me,
thanked me, shook my hand.

I felt like an American that night.

Came to this country just
a boy, ten years earlier,
dust of the Sonora still
hot between my toes.

That was my first job, scarce
out of high school.
I'll never forget how kind
he was, how like a friend.

Bobby.

Twenty-four hours later,
I knelt there, cradling his head
on the cold kitchen floor
while his blood and brains spilled out.

I couldn't wash my hands for days.

Transgendered Ex at Son's Birthday Party

I think to change into a t-shirt,
    something in which I can chase kids with water guns,
      something that disregards cleavage and shoulder.
You arrive in a pretty little dress.
    It's edgy, a sweetheart neckline
      white with black trim and little crickets and bees
      perched about.
And those legs, the sort I've always wanted — long and lean.
    Why do boys always have the best legs?
      No saddlebags or cellulite, but smooth exclamation points.
Your legs point up beyond the flared skirt to your new chest
that I don't recognize.
    I adjust my shirt, the one I will not change out of, the one
    that is not unisex.
    And I reapply my colored lip balm, the same as yours, I gave
    you last Winter.
I give you a hug and you feel dewy, like a woman glistening.
Never before good at forgetting, I cannot now remember what
it was like to be yours.
I hesitate when introducing myself as his mom, with a glance
towards you.
    I see your mascara as a challenge and think that I should
    accent my eyes more.
      More feminine and brave, I see you as a Goddess, as
      supernatural as real.
I wish I kept that man I met after you left, the one with the
linear thoughts
    who told me that women are from Venus and I talk too
    much.

But only briefly, just to have someone to steady me for a
moment.
I avert my eyes as you bend to pick up a candle, a shock of electric blue peeking out.
I imagine the men I might meet — Tom with the spiky
beard that might rub
a rash on my face when we kiss. Glenn who rides a
motorcycle.
You embrace your son and it looks like a parent holding
birthday wishes close to the boy.
No change can render that image unforgettable and for a
moment again I am yours.

On Becoming the Church Bag Lady

I wear him on my sleeve
I still feel him
Holding me down
So heavily
Not like a brick
But like a gallon of milk
A fresh bag of groceries
A newborn child
We carry so much weight on our shoulders
We can't even call the bag ladies bag ladies anymore
Because we've all turned into bag ladies
You carry your past on your back
Your future in your hands
And you're not even sure where to put your present
You lose it so often
It seems less and less important
Eventually it will become part of your past
Like your scars
And his hands
Eventually you will have too many bags to carry
And secrets to keep
And stories to remember
But eventually you will be okay
Stronger
No longer fueled by your hate for him
No longer weighed down
By all that you carry with you
Everyday

CL BLEDSOE

A Kind of Spring

The best time to fall in love
is when you share your greatest fear
with someone who isn't listening.

There's a decent chance that
will become your newest
greatest fear. There's no point

in letting it shift to anger; who
do you think will listen to that?
Close your eyes and run as fast

as you can into oncoming traffic.
Whoever stops to save you, marry
them. If no one stops—let's be honest,

no one will—at least you've
made good time home. When someone
talks about the weather on an

elevator, don't believe them until
they offer a ring. There are spies
everywhere. When your heart stops,

it probably means you're dead. Don't
worry. All winter, your joints
have ached with chill. When summer

comes, you open your windows to
sneeze at the world. There's war
outside, but no one calls it that. If they

do, consider baking something for
them. The brown haired men with
accents all call you sir, and the women

snap at their children to make way
when you pass. Smile. Say something
soothing. Step into the mud. If you can

think of a way to feel better about all
this, of a way to stop the meanness
of the heart, please let me know.

Breathing Away the Darkness

At night, lights appear, unseen amongst
daytime's dominating sun.
Scattered bits of moon peering curiously
through window slats.
The warmth of some adjoining room
creeping in under a doorway;
a guest that stays the night and leaves
soundlessly in the morning.
The passing of headlights chasing fate down
an anonymous highway.
These, the nightlights counting time,
until the sunrise,
keeping pace with silent lungs,
Lifting and lowering,
breathing away the darkness
into some brighter being.

Two Poems and a Haiku

The divorce.
The final chapter of our union
tells of bone deep chagrin-
the dumb utter of
'I feel statements'
plays itself like a mantra,
useless invocations found
in the crumpled leaflets
from the therapist's office.
The pointed questions
from our guilty mouths
forces a sober thought through;
we felt the cold walk in
but we never felt the warmth walk out.
The silent stare between us
measures the immeasurable,
a gulf of indifference grows-
it's time to close dead eyes,
and move on from this grave.

A heart.
On a Sunday evening
she noticed mold growing
within the divots and cracks
of this old rotted thing—
plucked from her chest
by her own hand
she buried it in the trash
alongside burnt letters
and bad eggs,

muttering to herself
that it was too rancid
to keep.

Dinner with the folks.
My mother simmers oxtails
and hollers like a kettle—
high blood pressure and anxiety,
nothing is ever good enough,
she fans herself with a dish cloth
while she squawks about ingrates
and too much gristle.

Beneath brown eaves
my father smokes in silence,
he watches moss grow over a stone.

Mire.
Drifting morning fog;
rivulets gather and wash
over broken trees.

Retirement.
Tired hands fumble
with the clasp of an old bra—
elm trees groan at night.

Items in a Neighborhood

Flag of America
Hanging behind a sign
That says, "Thank you Jesus."

Holy patriotism

Support the overseer w/ a gun
DON'T RUN
In spite of not having 1

Blue cross/red blood/white face

Tired fabric
Rests on ancient representation

Loyalists singing hymns

Guarded by a pentagram w/ a gun
DON'T RUN
In spite of not having one

White flash/blue light/red eyes

The God
Embraces played ideology

Dat' Ol' Time Religion

You be the Legion surrounded by a wall w/ a gun
DON'T RUN

In spite of not having I.

Red Objectives/White Lies/Blue Reality

Goddesses Incognito

Underneath
the drab,
the daily,
we are passionate goddesses parading in
spangles
glinting jewels
shimmering cloth
that mirror our enticing hips.
Underneath ragged watchcaps,
we are tender goddesses
crowned in
headwraps
tiaras
mantillas
bandanas
that accentuate our nobility.
Underneath blowsy t-shirts,
blazing ads in giant orange letters scrawled across our chests,
we are opulent goddesses wrapped in a splendor of
plaids
kente
batik —
rich in colors that males
don't even know the names
much less the significance of.
Behind plastic face masks that claim to guard us from infection,
we are amusing goddesses
roaring out the music of joy
harmonies of silver giggles
cymbal crashes of belly laughs

organ peal guffaws
in happy certainty of our right to
pleasure given,
pleasure taken.
We are hidden where you expect us least.
Show us due homage
and we may flash you a glimpse
into our hidden realm.
Or we may not.
The unexpected entices goddesses
most of all.

My Ancestors

My ancestors picked cotton
Worked hard stacked brick by brick
The old say the young
Just scroll the mouse
Facebook Instagram and click
They call them the instant
Microwave generation
Smoke some marijuana
Now on high school graduation
No job dedication
But hand eye coordination
Quick on that Playstation
I, ME, ME
I can't wait for the
iPhone, new Playstation, Wii
My ancestors just wanted to be free
Free like
Your night and weekend cell phone plan
Got welts on their back for being African
When they wanted to be treated like a MAN!
Now we drown our sorrow in beer from
Big K liquor store
Because we know we came here on a boat
We aint get no ticket for.

One Night Ghost

Under a chipped summer moon
I haunt the front yard of the house
we once called home. From the outside

through the warp of glass, I see you
with her, dancing past the picture
window. You could be us, gliding

past the coffee table, your hips
swaying like flowers, naked skin
offered without thought or bruising.

Such petal-soft touching once lived
with us—the back porch swing where we
rocked while its old bones creaked, cracks

in the linoleum that tripped
us between stove and sink, the grill
where you flipped burgers, cooked corn, burned

the letters you had once written
me. Back in the car I breathe, wait
for my ghost to quit its stalking.

Haiku

Haiku Haiku
haiku moment —
most pure
before words form

swallowing cherry blossoms...
will I compose haiku
with a japanese heart?

loon skimming still lake
above its own image —
wordless poem

soul of the poet

soul of the Friend
rice paper waiting for the brush

[note: Friend is the formal term for a Quaker]

a canoe

a haiku

each floating on reflection

Spirit Haiku

journeying through
the heart of god —
our paddles silently dip and swing

climbing the mountain trail
I hear echoes
of footsteps not yet taken

I see machu picchu ... and
the stones turn to blood
and rush through my veins

fog steals up from behind
startles me
then holds me in its arms

her heart soars like a midnight loon...
calling, calling
each quivering soul

swirling along the winding path
leaves and breezes . . .
yet   where to?   where from?

stones of the old monk's floor,
worn smooth but never cold —
his feet afire...

Ocean

I've got insomnia
again. I lay awake
for hours, listening
to the fan whirl
as my thoughts swim
round and round to you.
You're six hours
behind so when I can't
sleep we text, the quiet
pinging of your incoming
message the whale song
I listen for. We tread
carefully but each message
has an undercurrent. We wade
deeper into these waters, aware
of the rip tide threatening below.
I split my life between two
oceans, split my body between
two pairs of hands – floating
toward the current, my heart
underwater, the hands
capable of saving
or drowning me.
Shelter
His voice is a storm
I've learned to weather.
He lives in a state of tornado
watches and hurricane warnings.
The sun hidden by storm
clouds for so long my skin

has grown pale and translucent.
A ghost-girl growing cold,
my blue blood pumping slowly.

I zip up my raincoat, my parka,
my all-weather jacket. I brace
myself for the torrent
of words and rage he'll throw
at me. The anger raining down,
stinging my skin, invisible
cuts that will never quite heal
but will sing with pain every
time lightning strikes.

I've started seeking shelter elsewhere,
finding warmth and words from another
mouth. His hands never curl into thunder-
fists, his tongue never spins
an uncontrolled storm. I shed
my layers, find the sun in his skin.
Lay content in his clear skies.

Norman Rockwell Thanksgiving

My mother framed the Rockwell painting.
That image of matriarch in white apron
setting down white platter
with turkey large enough to feed
all the smiling faces at the table.

Everyone's eyes gleam with affection
anticipating a meal as delectable as manna.

Every mouth is happy to heap praise
as generously as they spoon mashed potatoes.

No one longs to be anywhere else
with anyone else.

"It's the way it's supposed to be,"
my mother often said with red nose
and wet handkerchief
as year after year
her dining room bore no resemblance
to Norman Rockwell's painting,
particularly the pleased patriarch
standing behind his wife.

The picture hangs on my wall, too,
as I sit at an undressed table
to eat cold cereal with a book
written by a family therapist
happy to explain
why idealized images
damage self-esteem.

Hopper's Diner Second Shift: Reflection on the Mood of "Nighthawks" (1942)

For the waitress behind
the counter, there is a serenity
that pretends to come
with the end of the day,

when the sunlit crowds have left
and a few stragglers clack
heels down a dusky
film noir side street,

when the second sitting
dinner crowd has disappeared
and the guy at the end
of the counter sipping coffee,

hoping the waitress would bend over
in front of him, her puckered
blouse the only sex he'd get
for the night, finally leaves,

when late shift nighthawks alight
and the matte black of night
fills the background
behind the neon,

then her shift is done and she
says "G'night" to Cal the late guy,
goes home, undresses alone,
lets out the cat to prowl midnight,

and crawls into bed feeling
the end of the day settle over her body
like a flannel blanket of armor
against the bedlam of the day.

If John Waters Hung Out in Reston

He'd live in our townhouse, with the filthiest bathroom alive—
a rust hole in the sink so big it'll leak
all over the floor if you fill it, and a
cardboard Elvis cutout who wears his golden
suit on our stairwell. He'll scare the crap
out of you if you're not warned. Instead of chickens
we have a family of finches nesting above
our deck. Their bird house has a Tennessee
license plate draped, bent over the top for
a roof. The daddy warbles from atop
a long dead gas grill. There's a hole
in that too, right where we used to connect
the propane tank. Johnny would love that we
could burn the whole motherfucker down.
All these animals, chirping and screwing, making
animal babies to live in this nest. The daddy
finch has two calls—one a ventriloquist
act he does with dinner in his beak.
His other is a warning. "Get the fuck out,"
when we're sitting out with morning coffee.
I can't tell if he's speaking to the babies
or to us. They start out shitty fliers,
dodging the owls and hawks, or the occasional
fat ass squirrel who hops from our moldy hammock
stealing food from their feeder. In
the end, their wings grow thicker like our skin.
They leave, maybe to return, maybe not.
No predictable plot. Johnny would like that too.

Pergola

In loving memory of Arminda Agusto, our Vovó.

I never grew out of cookies
and milk
I grew in.
Someone reflective,
not out loud.
Even behind the smoke,
I saw wheels turn and wondered
where had you gone?

Perhaps it was to the oceans of your youth,
a brave island against the rough Atlantic
where the Portuguese language carves out its own beauty,
through a faith and knitted family.
Your arms glide through the pool
like you sliced tomatoes into salad,
how light cut through the grape vine pergola.

That trip we took together to the Azores
opened my eyes to the backbone you were
a set of vertebrae to hold a family strong.
A woman with many joys taken
at all hours after siesta, with coffee
and cake in the midnight talking hours.
Laughter that woke me with a smile.

I knew then what I realize now
like the smoke we fade.
Dissipate into the atmosphere

touching brief lives,
impart advice.
Grace that layers beneath –
a foundation on which I stand
wavering in this mourning.

One Step Down

Toward the New Year, that late December,
we parked the car near the old Sealtest Plant
just off Pennsylvania a block down from
Washington Circle where, since 1860, the
General has sat, always astride his mount,
determined in his slave holding gentility,
as the world spun out and
away from him.

And in that block the world was spinning
away from us as Joe, the proprietor, gruffly
welcomed us with an icy stare as we descended
into the gloom stepping down that small increment
to the One Step Down which was jazz and junky
central in that part of town and, accepted there,
hippie juicers, we sort of fit in without the
peculiarities of those habits related to a
noble musical profession so filled with
prophets and fallibility.

Charles "Yard-Bird" Parker wailed from the jukebox
and we could never figure out where those ancient
45's came from that never seemed to wear out as
generations of drunks poured in their quarters and
"Strange Fruit" came with a bitter crop defined as
the place peeled back all assumptions.

The secretive white Georgetown addicts filled the bar
stools most nights while the student types, sitting in
the ancient wooden booths along the right wall, got

pitchers of beer for $2.50 or so and nodded sagely to
the always lovely waitresses who sometimes had what
you needed for exams in one of the beer apron front
pockets where those essential study aides, the "black
beauties," were kept, two or three of those waking
a kid up for a day or two, this joint being known
as sort of a "one stop shop" for this sort of thing.

Philosophers all we raged far into the night till last call
touching the dreams of those real hipsters from the 50's,
they still an echo that we just caught, some of us skeptical
of the bright colors and vague assumptions of our age,
attracted to the darker hues down here,
just that final step, that last step, those
few steps down that might penetrate
the fog and make the world
clear at last.

And just before the lights came up I sat there
with a brilliant friend, later to succumb to
religion, who for now was as gloomy as a
Russian poet fresh from Gulag, giving me
that old Mandelstam look of doom while
pronouncing life shit as I took issue with
his threats of self-harm based on a violent
passion for a woman far advanced in maturity,
if not years, someone he just could not handle.
In the end Old Baby Jesus saving him,
he settling for that as slowly,
from that night,
we drifted apart.

But for then, in the listless light of the early
hours we ventured out, covered by the
infernal glow of an all-night fire,
braced more for action than for

more words, working out the
dangers as we, ever carefully
calibrated and backlit,
stepped into the city
and continued to
mark our time.

Statue in the Shallows

Odd. Just plain odd. No other word for it.
It's hard to see, against the backdrop
of beech and brush at the edge of the river.
Fisherfolk stare across the water—pondering

why a statue would be planted in such a spot.
Two reedy posts for a base, a torso in the mold
of a bloated football, the top an L-shaped pole
slightly angled. Odd spot for artwork—waterfowl

are the area's main visitors. Mallards fly low,
leapfrogging each other. An osprey jets down,
hooks a fish, leaves. Every 30 seconds,
a cormorant slides feet-first to a watery landing,

like a baseball player trying to beat the tag
at third. Sounds are few, faint: plop of a lure
breaking the dull green surface, soft rhythm of paddles
as kayakers mosey downstream. In two bends

they'll spy the iconic obelisk of the Washington
Monument. The only other urban inkling,
now and then, is a silver Boeing 757 lumbering
toward a landing—like the cormorant, feet-first.

The statue is tiny compared to bronze equestrians
who inhabit parks and traffic circles across the city;
curiously, they include Joan of Arc. Someone
with a strong arm—and stronger conceit—might hurl

a rock across the Potomac at the statue; it would fall short.
That thought takes off instantly as *frawk, frawk*
breaks the stillness, the statue sprouts colossal wings
and, graceful as a ballerina, the great blue heron lifts skyward.

All You Remember

Climb the stairs. Take the call.
Stand by the old green chair.
Don't sit down.
Hear your mother say
It's cancer.
Don't answer right away.
Clamp down your fear
before you speak.
Grip the green chair's frame.
You only get one chance:
say the right things right.
Your hands and voice can't shake.
Take the dress you wore that day.
Throw it out. Tell it
you don't care
it is the color
of peach blossoms. Throw out the chair
and the photos of your mother, younger, your age,
slender in the blossom-colored dress she wore
before she passed it on to you.
Regret this even as you do it.
Do it. You must
throw out everything,
throw in anything to fill the pit in time
opened by your hesitation. Ask: What did you say
to ease your mother's fear? What did you say
to ease her grief? What did you say? What
did you say?

The pause between your words
and her reply
is all you remember.

Refugee

Fear is in your bread
and you must choke it down.
To think of home—
the courtyard with its red filigreed rug,
the peel-paint walls, how the breeze with its tang
of the Khabur River touched your just-cut hair
as you curled up, writing in your diary—
starts the slide of grief, the thundering
that blocks out sound, pulls
a knife across each breath until
you drag your body like a sack,
walking with others
toward the border.
But something rises up,
wants to live:
> *I won't be that man sitting*
> *on his burned porch, face a lace of cuts,*
> *waiting in rain for death.*
Shut away now the images of home,
like your diary with its leather straps.
Preserve your young life.
Eat your bread.

The Story of My Father

He spoke seven languages and was never allowed to leave the country.
He'd gone to school in Paris, which made him an enemy of the people.
I'm sorry, but this is the only way I know to tell the story. He had
a family—a wife and daughter—but that is for someone else to tell.
He was a translator during the Cold War. When the big countries
wanted to talk, he would translate their languages.
He loved languages. He loved words. He wanted artistic license,
he wanted to say beautiful things in those beautiful tongues.
But there was nothing he could do, their conversations disintegrating,
and he never changed a word, not intentionally, for 32 years.
By then his daughter had left for school in a foreign country, to study
languages. His wife was working as a doctor in North Africa.
He had the dog, Lily, who ate with him at the table. He served her
on the good china, and she seemed to understand all seven languages.
Then one day, after Lily grew ill and died, it happened.
The diplomat said, "We will not stand for this! We have boats full
of heat-seeking missiles ready to destroy you." He translated,
     unwavering,
"We will send boats full of flowers on your country's birthday."
The other party looked bewildered, "We can annihilate your half of
     the world."
He said, "The mothers in your country are the most beautiful in
     the world."
After a few murmurs the diplomats figured it out. It would take more
than language to fix their conversation. They decided he'd
     gone senile,
retired him at 62. He wasn't sad to go, but he had nothing
left to do—everything had worked up to that one moment.
Seven months later he died, before the end of the war and before
any end was in sight. I sometimes feel sad he couldn't see the solution,

but it wasn't about flowers or mothers anyway, and now a
    new war's on,
one he couldn't translate for. He only knew seven languages.

Patriotism Reconsidered

My anthem is the serenade of birds,
sung without regard for map lines
delineating human assumption of dominion
over that which cannot be possessed,
and I will not pledge allegiance to,
or defend a flag of illusory freedom.

As the sun greets each day,
I will bravely stand up—against
racism, gendered hate, and xenophobia.

I will join in solidarity
with those who block pipelines
and protest gun violence,
those who feed the hungry
and work to stop the school
to prison pipeline,
and with every person who works
for the common good.

Solemnly I swear not to tolerate
the revision of history to fit
a fraudulent justification for
perpetual war or
wanton destruction of Earth.

This is my oath of citizenship,
because to do anything else is treason.

Driving to Juniata

for David Hutto

Up there's the interstate, peeping through trees.
Down here among hollows, satellite dishes,
a man on his deck guzzles beer, wishes
he were driving that highway. His fancy speeds
past the graveyard of riding mowers, the three-
foot ceramic gnome squatting on the lawn
beside a cabin whose mailbox reads "Yablonski" –
speed's his algorithm for life, for freedom.
I don't know where America lives, but I know
in my bones she's down here, among red-lacquered
barns, weed-choked byways, plank bridges.
She bleeds through the landfills, the tiered ridges
of doublewides, the hand-lettered placards
with directions to Jesus: be patient. Go slow.

Dark Energy

—for the parents of the children at Sandy Hook

Notice what you remember this day:
how clean the air smells,
how warm it is for winter,
how you hoped it would be snowing.
Notice how bare the trees are,
black birds perched
in the empty branches,
cracked ice on a puddle.
Notice lips, hair, skin,
fingertips, tongue,
the place in the sky
you saw the first star
last night and closed your eyes,
from habit, wishing, wishing, wishing.
Notice what you won't remember:
how quiet it was the moment
after the gunshots,
that the screaming
sounded like coyotes in the desert.
Notice blur of smoke,
river of blood,
skin stuck to walls, missing faces.
Notice your question:
why must a coffin
hold a child,
why not rocks, mud,
burnt wind, even water?
Notice there is no waking from this dream,

the sky will always be this dark.
the only living will be living
on the edge of a black hole.
Notice a million stars exploding daily.

The Cancer Fairy

It was a small dark body, like a mouse.
Unemployed, it still drove the car,
pushing the TV out the passenger-side door,
yellow chyme and bile the color of grass,
like the time the Ferris Wheel made the little kids cry
at the Okoboji of slow dancing
There are things you can do with music
or, as in this case, with your voice.
Dense as fudge
it pullulated with margins outside
the half a permitted millimeter
of tissue-wrapped meat.
Tender slits healed as
she cried out for corporate capital,
offed her white negligee and wig,
disinviting them from her gondola,
it and its sleeper cells, daughter cells
for whom she had, unknowingly peeled
carrots and quartered pears in the Denver
of the stockyards.
We all came to hold her hand,
the dancer, the flight attendant, the nurse,
the teacher, the librarian,
all dripping tears
silly with love, the light
shedding like a dog in August,
an old dog.

Island

She would cry every time we put her in the carriage. That was all right, and the way I had to lean sideways to make her sleep. Her soft breath on my face. Smelled like waste. My back would heal and she would nurse. My nipples still blue when the sound of the ocean stopped. Sometimes the trees bend toward me and I'll feel something like it. Or taste it just before. The gold dripping off the leaves, just before it sweetens and betrays.

From Let the Wind Push us Across

Tent

Sometimes in the morning,
before opening my eyes,
I dream of our tent,
that tiny green dome.
From behind its walls
thin as skin, I hear birds,
leaves, a brush of wind.
I yearn for that waking,
that once tethered dawn when
unzipping the door
I leaned into the world.

James Hampton, The Throne of the Third Heaven of the Nations Millennium General Assembly (ca. 1950–1964)

Tossing away sandwiches,
chewing gum, cigarettes,
he made his heaven from wrappers,
commerce's carapace. Who would discard
the meat of the thing: shake out
the book and bow to
the empty jacket, feed on
Baggies and shells, expect
twenty-four blue robes to rise
and offer a requiem? Recall, then,
that this temple of trash was made
in a garage: a heavenly vehicle,
we, entering, fuel.

I Want to Write About the N-Word

I want to write about nipples even though
no word is safe I write about nipples
because they make me uncomfortable
and the things I cannot touch
with my eyes look good in black ink.
Because black ink is a private part
I can hide behind a white wall and ask
why our nipples turn dark and moody while nursing
and all nipples turn the same shade of brown
but not blushing under exposure as if
color changes the social cue
unembarrassed and maybe fuck you.
I want to know why nipples feel foreign
thus darkened and why it's dangerous.
I want to admit I've never seen the nipples
of a black nursing mother and my world
stays smaller as a result as a world without
color is a world without changes in nipples
so I speak about nipples for part of the planet
while all other sisters' nipples remain
obscured from me. Other nipples.
I don't want to Other nipples. I want
to acknowledge that nursing alters nipples,
the pink/tan/pert learns to undulate
whorls beyond the realm of seashells,
inexplicable curls and I want to write
about nipples like it's natural
because nipples are natural and I am so much
socialization conditioned to fear the change
in body parts. To cover what grows un-young.

I'm sick and tired seeing the disproportionate appearance of
Anglo/American nipples at the expense of *everyotherwoman.*
We are sum-one. And yet—I cannot write about nipples because
no other flesh is cut from the same cloth. I can NOT
because they are different but I want to because
they are my mother's. And I am my mother's
daughter plus *everyotherlivinggirlnipple*
writing the shit we shouldn't say.

MILES DAVID MOORE

To Fatslug, the World is a Voynich Manuscript

Surrounding Fatslug, the unreadable:
puffy letters melting into each other
on the sides of rail cars, hip-hop hieroglyphics
sprayed onto random walls and sidewalks.

Growing between the cracks of this alphabet
are weeds of uncertain growth and scabby bloom.
No botanist has ever acknowledged them.
No sane one would even try.

Fatslug emerges from his doorway crevice
into a street filled with cuneiform faces,
gazing at concrete as he tries to hide
the strange, indecipherable growth of his heart.

Epilogue

I hate you with the sharpness of the edges of a Viking's teeth
I hate you from every part of my body – from my ankles, my
knees and my throat
I hate you from the feet of all my ancestors
and from my heartbeat from when I was an ocean fish
You are a force who brings innocent branches down with a crash
Under the guise of kindness and support
You came to me
dressed up like a kind old lady
begging for an apple
I gave you my orchard
You said you loved to coach
But for you Losing was an all the time thing
You paid this poet with your darkest habits
You coach your arm in fistfights with the angels
Your other arm, good, stays defeated
Locked up in your stupid cage
Throw your fist, punch the sky
kill the birds and watch me fly
From the concrete mess you make,
I take the rubble, the hate
A bulk so heavy I have flung it at every other guy,
hurting my own back.
You made me your heart's punching bag
I'm haunted – flinching from your ghost attacks
Exhausted
I have wrung out all the sweat from all the clothes I've suffered in
Since your last emotional blow years ago
You left me exhausted in a field of your own personal battles –
And now I remain victorious in my knowledge

I didn't ever do anything wrong
I'm just a poet who needs to sing her song
while you remain back there slinging back drinks
in that bar, you know the one, where on sunny days,
pigs are brought to roast

The Beginning of Prayer

My father, tangled in the height of adolescence,
wept outside Old Saint Paul's Church as spring died,
reading Desiderata. The poem lay inscribed
in rock at the rear of the church, where
he counted his blessings. The sky,
he told me, was angry, angrier than most,
and I imagined billowy Michelangelos
swollen with inconsolable rain.

I was eight when he told the story late one night,
after dinner, after all candles had been blown out.
He stroked my back as I lay on his stomach,
burying myself into his large body, thinking
This is the moment I'm supposed to remember.
I watched his movements, listening to his pulse,
for what was coming, for what would soon be
the trickling of my own prayer.

One afternoon, my father awoke to a pounding
in his temples, to a plum-colored bruise
the size of a mango, spreading across his head
like a puddle. As his brain bled, my mother
stood outside the door at the hospital, waiting,
because this is what doctors recommend.
To wait. My sister looked out onto the parking lot,
the window streaked with black rain.

After he began to walk again, wobbling back
into the house with an almost-familiar smile,
I thought of what he had said all those years ago.

I thought of the swelling of the clouds, how
I thought it would never stop raining
after he'd come inside, carrying candlelight
that bloomed in every room,
and that I would never feel safe again
for as long as I prayed.

Kitchen Fire

In the photo of the kitchen fire,
We are dressed for Christmas:
Me in a flammable hand-me-down jacket,
Her in her costume jewelry
And her Edward Scissorhands t-shirt.

The scene is blurred and blue with smoke, since,
In the photo of the kitchen fire, the fire itself
Is still in progress, burning on in the background,
Small but insistent.

The explosion has not happened yet,
in the photo of the kitchen fire—
Soon the door of the toaster oven will blow out
Like a bistro window in an action movie.
The food on the counter behind us
Will glitter with bites of glass.

We are not moving
In the photo of the kitchen fire, or
At least we are not leaving.
No, I am wringing my hands
And my eyes are all whites and alarm,
And my mother's mouth is twisted,
Like she's trying not to laugh, or cry,
Or both—with her, it's often both—
And she is turning me toward her, away
From the blaze in the background.

There is no fire extinguisher
In the photo of the kitchen fire;
Perhaps my boyfriend
Had gone to get it. Still my mother and I
Are not leaving. My sister
Has reached for her camera.

On Other Birds

Through the harsh whistle of a
bullying Blue Jay from the feeder,
the Common Yellowthroat's
wichity-wichity-wichity,
we find our own through bill and tap
and rhythmic drumming on drainpipe,
bone against bone.
So much more is said
when the yard is
quiet...
So much more spoken
between   wings.

Speaking to the Rain

We can speak to the rain,
but it does not say anything to us.
"Why are you so strong?
Why do you want to flood us?"
we ask it. But it only pushes
harder toward the ground,
forming mud, overflowing
the creek. We don't understand
why it will never answer,
when we can hear its voice
in its fall from the sky, tinkling
sound of drizzle, the thumps
of downpours. Walking into
the open, our clothes are drenched,
they stick to our body, becoming
almost translucent with water.
We find canoes and inflatable rafts,
afraid we might have to float
to survive. Maybe there is
a common language we're missing?
Maybe the rain speaks Esperanto,
maybe it's an unidentified tongue?
In translation books, we sift through
Mongolian and French, but are not
able to find one. What we fear most
is that wind will arrive, and then we'll
have to translate further. Except
we know that it's always spoken to us
in English, in nightmares, where it blows
down alphabets, turns words into screams.

Working Farm for Sale

The hives have gotten through another year—
I'm sure you've heard of the alternative.
Buy soon and you can have the Holsteins here.
No guarantee of how much milk they'll give.
Tobacco had the soil worn out before
Some fallow years and compost brought it back.
The orchard yields enough to eat and store,
Or make a batch of your own applejack.
Of course, a price like this can't buy perfection.
Feel free to ask me questions and take notes.
You get the feed lot's smell from that direction.
The stream is muddied by a neighbor's goats.
Let's step inside. The gun rack's over there.
This far from town, you'll want a gun somewhere.

Suitcase

In the end, you have no suitcase.

The ticket is one-way only, very expensive, caro, precious.

You arrive on the side of a hill which has dared to assert
    its contours
into the life of endless blue sky
and you sit next to the little shed with its rusted tools,
find the rabbit carcass drying in a gorge of light.

You've left home with instructions to love
your body, your ankles crumbling beneath you.

Your suitcase, navy blue, like all the others
is carefully zippered around the loves of your heart,
your neck of arteries and veins folded neatly over your pants
    and scarves
the ones with the silver thread flowers
and the ones with the outlines of petroglyphs
the freckled bowl you bought somewhere
and nestled into the fabric with your spotted hands.

In the end, you will dream of packing your suitcase.
You will ask someone you love to get it down from the attic
even though you have no attic
and you did not know that you could feel so much love
for a stained undershirt and a chipped necklace

or your own blood warming in the dark.

. . . as if he were holding the sea in his black hands,
as if, after giving him all that power, she now could give
him pity and consolation . . .
from "The Same Moon Above Us" by Gerald Stern

Lament for Bob Dylan

Lament, lament for Hibbing, for Duluth,
    lament for Marquette, for Munising, for the Sault;
Let me lament the raw earth, its skin scraped off;
Lament for the grass pulled up by the roots;
Lament, lament for the pure child, the pure dirt;
Let me lament the sheer rain of words—each pure
    note harnessed to the right word;
Let me lament, let me lament, let me lament for the electrician's
    son with the sizzling hair, song searing the mouth, cracking
    the lips, lament caught in the throat;
Let me lament the swirl of ash on the tongue, the charred word;
Let me lament the eagle's beak rotted with poison, lament blowing
    through the nose, wind in a ruin;
Blistered tear, smooth cheek—let me lament the downy hair
    on the young neck, the suspicious eyes, the walking debt;
Let me lament the dumb repetition of hunger.
    faithful generations of want;
Lament, lament for the gate open and shut;
Lament, lament for the locked box of luck;
Lament for the rain both inside and out;
Lament for the money borrowed and stunned;
For the rank cruelty and unintended harm;
For the useless car and the wailing fire truck—
    for the *phony false alarm*—
Lament for the stiff mask strayed from the shelf;

and for the electric son plugged in, playing himself;
For the risky kitchen where you freeze, where you bake—
    weep for real pain—the phantom ache—
Lament for the authorities, for the agents, for the brakeman,
    for the promoters, lament for the undertaker, the agitators,
    the commissioners, the free-loaders, lament for the sword
    swallower, the throat-borrower, for the war horse, the riot
    squad, lament for the scentless roses;
Lament for the pillar of salt corroding in the sun, he thought he had
    everything, he never looked back—he didn't know what he'd done;
And for wise incorruptible love—gone like ice—gone like air—
    lament for the quivering bridge;
Lament, lament for the angel visions of Johanna—were they hers?
    Were they his? Were they mine? Were they yours?
Lament for the harm done unto you, the harm you did;
Lament for the love done wrong, time mislaid, scratched
    face at the window, rain tracks on the pane;
Wolf moans at the blue door—jowl sagging, smoldering eye—his one
    song—his sole idea of order;
And woe sing the wholly free, released from the strings of the body;
Let me lament the busted windows of the sea;
And for the ship stalled at the shore, deranged harpoon,
    impostor cabin boy, manic crew;
Lament for the engine, lament for the sail, for the bowline,
    for the mast, lament for the whale;
And the delusional captain adrift in the dunes— ·
    his fevered pockets—his drunken shoe—
Fire thirsts, unquenchable, guzzling the parched air,
    tomorrow's long past, the hours rust—
And the little boy lost in the blinding snow, bitter cold, smoking eyelids,
    fire, the fire full of holes;
Lament for the north country, jumping off place, end of the
    world, mine's closed, the borderline's blurred;
For the bootless weatherman, the aimless wind—
    and for the ghost of electricity whistling its scorched hymn;
Lament, lament for the ground, insects that play there, delicate

snake in the weeds, the purposeful ants, lizards,
turtles, everything that breathes;
Lament for the National Guard guarding the wrong door, for the
bored slave,
the *homesick sailors,* half-lit ladies, escape artist,
crumbled fortress, cold Joker, traitor kiss;
Let me lament the strangled voice cut off of the vine,
lament for the words that have shriveled and died;
Lament for the homeless, the ruthless, the witless, the clueless,
the deathless, the reckless, the eyeless, the foolish;
Let me lament the pale night, the black daytime,
lament for the feckless nickel, the friendless dime;
Let me note the little red hen's lament, and the evil step-sisters'
lament, and
the great ape and the little elves dancing their lament;
Lament, lament for this old man, his house full of knick-
knacks, his single
thumb, his dog Bingo, his nameless furious wife;
Lament, lament for the mutilated mice, the triumphant cheese, lone-
some cornbread, juicy frog, the innocent knife;

Let me lament, let me lament, let me lament for the hoodlum
persuaders
of song—scattered dust—desolate carnival boys, their wild
high-wire rhymes, their sisters' speechless science;
Lament, lament for the low ringing of the law;
Lament for the tambourine giant, the silver saxophones and the
flutes;
Lament for Jack-a-Diamonds, for Gypsy Davy, for Mr. Jones
"Don't-Know-What's-
Happening-Do-You," for the cocky punks, the plucky
scoundrels, the scorned lovers, the jealous monk;
Lament for the city of truth spoken in song;
Pity the shadow of the laughter of youth—burned—gone—
their god knocked

down—the ikon broken—rattle bag of bones and polka dot rag—already
the prophets mourn—the robin falls mute—and the dove—and
the raven—black fire flailing her unfeathered wings—their illegible
scrawl—soft white underbelly of the brain—tick of the heart hung in its sac,
roiling, swollen—golden drop of sweat;
And the windowsill and the tattered ceiling—
And the cowboy angel astride his cloud-horse, twirling his lariat candle;
And the renegade physicist fiddler, fiddling in anger;
Naked emperor at the edge, howling for his lost dominion, his soldier-
clowns stuck in the coffin phonebooth;
And his junkyard bed, its skeleton mattress, his black tooth;
And Maggie's farm, what she grew there, her lunatic ma, her raging
    pa, her cerebral servant, her well-scrubbed floor;
And Rita and Annie, and Mona and Louise, all the saints in the
    penitentiary;
Let me lament for the 18, for the 30, the 50 years' wait;
Lament for the price you paid—what you had to say—what you
    were offered, what you didn't get straight;
Let me note every lament and lament each note:
                                        Let me lament

            the choked wind, the dry rain
            the shattered hand and the wall
            a shell, a shard,   salt   sand
            unmanned man   the endless highway's end
            lion's breath   footsteps silent   abandoned name . . .
                            letmelament letmelament letmelament
                            letmelament letmelament, letmelament

Ah mama, can this really. . .
                                        the golden bead of sweat

letmelament, letmelament letmelament

I Too Would be a Stone

"The stone sinks, slow, unperturbed
To the river bottom
Where the fishes come to knock on it
And listen."
– Charles Simic

I too
would be a stone
if only I could
harden myself
enough I would
fit myself to
the palm of a boy
with bottles to break
or be kicked along
the curb by a sad
teenaged girl.
I would delight
in being skimmed
across the surface
of a pond happy
to then sink
silent past astonished
fishes if only
I could lose these
edges and take on
the weight.

JOHN MONAGLE

Tricycle Trip in the Mesilla Valley

When mother went to sleep
in the afternoon I pedaled
my tricycle by yards and houses
behind chain linked fences,
along paths beside dry ditches,
through a vacant lot,
across the sidewalk
before tracking on solid
yellow lines parting asphalt streets.

I pedaled toward the mesa,
cars rushed from ahead and behind.
Unconcerned about my danger,
I rode through the slow hours
before a mother left her son in the yard
and ran to stop my tricycle
on the yellow lines, straddling
her legs on the big wheel.
She carried me into her house
and fed me ice cream before calling
the police who arrived a short time after
and took me home in their cruiser.

Through the back window,
I tracked the sun's descent
through the final hours
to its splashdown. It sank
too quickly for me to join
others who went every day
to the evening party where

mothers put the sun to its sleep
while twilight children danced
on the tightrope of the horizon.

JESSICA WILDE

My Garden at Vetheuil

Mom took us to the National Gallery
when we'd had enough
of dolls, work-out videos
and make-your-own-popsicles.
"Which one is you?" she asked
and we stared up,
the walls whiter than at home.
The girl with the watering can?
The hula hoop?
The one that up close
is made of spots?

The little girl alone,
because she was blond,
and I was too, then.
The one who thought mom
wasn't looking
because she was so far ahead,
who could sit in a cardboard
moving box
in grass above her head
and be alone.

1880
Yellow spots with green,
shadows of moving flowers,
a little girl alone,
walking in front of the rest,
veering slightly to the left of the path,
her feet frozen in motion,

her youth trapped in one breath.

Monet's wrist trains my eyes
to recognize my face.
My face
with a mere suggestion of eyes
the color of my dress,
blue into green
peach into yellow
like the world with sun in your eyes.

Mom chose this postcard
years later,
to write me from Walter Reed,
when I would clorox the kitchen
before bed,
when I would sit on my floor
late in the night
and write Bible verses
on ripped up note paper,
tape them on my wall.

I taped the postcard too,
between rainbows are reminders of god
and a Teen-Bible cut-out
of how you look ahead when you carry coffee
so it doesn't spill—
a metaphor for looking to the future.
Now everyone has cancer
and metaphors of the energy
of color,
of beams bursting
through her body
dividing the cells
that divide too fast,
and her and me both

no longer suffice.
Mom rolls her eyes
at breast cancer patients,
lends them her books,
feeds them carrot juice.

But back then,
my Spanish teacher took me aside
when her mom died
and told me I understood
what it's like to ponder your mother's death.
I had no idea,
just accepted her jewelry,
let her call us in, one by one,
to choose the clip-on earrings
we had preferred most while playing dress-up,
the watch on a golden chain
that wound,
that my grandmother kept
in a box
in a plastic bag
with a rubber band around it,
padded with bandaids.

Two nurses,
girls in their twenties,
manned the radiation machine,
showed me a video
of the room behind the metal doors,
and the one nurse slapped the other.
"You're crossing your legs again,"
she said.
Crossing them makes varicose veins
like her mother had,
she explained.
Then, without a pause,

she pointed at my mother's feet,
coming out one end of the radiation machine
like groceries on the slowest moving
conveyer belt you've ever seen.

The Shallows

Oh for a life of sensations over thoughts!
                              -Keats

We passed into the shallows—
limbs slow wings—

the great world of days
something separable, irrelevant,

and minded only surface stars,
the dreaming elements.

So the stream held us: sensation fell
like water from our fingers,

shaped for an instant,
then returned—

and all we would attend to there
was summer sunlight, summer air.

Poet Bios

Alphabetical by last name.

The bios presented here are as first published with the poems included in the book in the magazine Bourgeon between 2007 and 2021.

Serena M. Agusto-Cox, a Suffolk University graduate, writes more vigorously than she did in her college poetry seminars. Her day job continues to feed the starving artist, and her poems can be read in Beginnings Magazine, LYNX, Muse Apprentice Guild, The Harrow, Poems Niederngasse, Avocet, Pedestal Magazine, and Mothers Always Write, among others. An essay also appears in H.L. Hix's Made Priceless and at Modern Creative Life, as does a Q&A on book marketing through blogs in Midge Raymond's Everyday Book Marketing. She also runs the book review blog, Savvy Verse & Wit , and is the founder of Poetic Book Tours.

Megan Alpert's poetry has appeared in Quarterly West, Sixth Finch, Contrary, Harvard Review, and others. Her journalism has been published online by The Atlantic, Smithsonian, The Guardian, and Foreign Policy, where she was a 2015-2016 fellow. She is the recipient of a reporting fellowship from the International Women's Media Foundation in 2016 and an Orlando Poetry Prize from A Room of Her Own Foundation in 2011.

Elizabeth Ashe is a sculptor and poet, who earned her MFA from the Mount Royal School of Art at the Maryland Institute College of Art, and an MFA in creative writing from Chatham University. Her public art projects have been on view at the Bemidji Sculpture Walk, Sukkahwood Festival, Art All Night DC, and the H St Festival. Ashe's poetry has appeared in Yellow Medicine Review, the Lavender Review, Vagabondage, and Badlands Literary Journal, among many others. Her work is included in Studio Visit Magazine, issue 46. Ashe lives in Washington, D.C., where she has an active studio practice. She is the Gallery Manager for DC Arts Center, and Exhibit and Event Technician at the Katzen Center, American University.

Jeffrey Banks, poetically known as "Big Homey" received his Masters in Divinity at Howard University. A regular fixture in poetry series in the DMV area, he's had opportunity to perform with major entertainment figures, and is the recipient of artist grants from the DC Commission on the Arts and Humanities. A finalist in the 2018 DC Poet Project he's also a poet educator and a fundraising and events consultant to non-profits. He's taken opportunities to bring his artist activism as an advocate against homelessness and in 2019 his poetry was featured in the National Association for Poetry Therapy anthology.

Anne Becker, the former poet laureate of Takoma Park, MD, is beginning her tenure as poet in residence at Pyramid Atlantic, a print-making and book arts studio and gallery in downtown Silver Spring, MD. She received an MA from the Writing Seminars, Johns Hopkins University, teaches at the Writer's Center in Bethesda, MD and offers tutorials for poets putting books together. Her books include The Transmutation Notebooks: Poems in the Voices of Charles and Emma Darwin and The Good Body (chapbook). Since 2001 she has led a special poetry workshop, Writing the Body, for those who have experienced life-threatening or chronic illness as patient, caregiver or family member.

CL Bledsoe is the author of twenty books, most recently the poetry collection Trashcans in Love, the short story collection The Shower Fixture Played the Blues, and the novel The Funny Thing About... He lives in Northern Virginia with his daughter and blogs, with Michael Gushue, at https://medium.com/@howtoeven.

Jody Bolz received her MFA from Cornell University, where she studied with A.R. Ammons. Her poems have appeared widely in such magazines as The American Scholar, North American Review, Ploughshares, Poetry East, and Prairie Schooner -- and in many literary anthologies. She is the author of A Lesson in Narrative Time (Gibson Books, 2004), the novella-in-verse Shadow Play (Turning Point Books, 2013), and The Near and Far (Turning Point Books, 2019). From

2002 to 2019, she edited the journal Poet Lore, founded in 1889.

Nancy Botta lives just outside Chicago with her husband, son, and a menagerie of tropical fish. A marketing concierge for a multinational conglomerate, Nancy has been publishing poetry in digital forums since the halcyon days of LiveJournal and AOL 4.0. Her most recent works have appeared in WINK: Writers in the Know; Soft Cartel; Three Lines Poetry; Furtive Dalliance; Haiku Journal; and other publications. Find her, and the remainder of her poetry, at https://rustedhoney.com/.

Laura Costas, a DC native, wonders if she is an artist often overtaken by words or a writer whose poems intermittently become pictures. She has won grants from the DC Commission on the Arts and the Montgomery County, MD Arts Commission, and an award from the American Institute of Graphic Arts. She is the author and designer of two books, Honest Stories published by DC's Gut Punch Press, and the autonomously produced Fabulae, Tales for an Age of Ambivalence.

Breanna DeSimone is a rising senior at Mount St. Mary's University pursuing a degree in English. She has worked as poetry editor for her college's literary journal Lighted Corners and her poetry has appeared in two issues of the annual publication. She was born in Springfield, Oregon but currently lives in Williamsburg, Virginia. Poetry allows her to share her perspective of the world and explore her passion for life. She also loves reading, traveling, and learning new things.

Anne Dykers is a poet and book artist in Silver Spring, MD. Her poems have appeared in Green Mountains Review and Ashen Meal. She has participated in numerous collaborative projects bringing together poets and visual artists at the Takoma Park Community Center, and her work has been exhibited at Pyramid Atlantic Arts Center in Silver Spring.

Kristin Kowalski Ferragut is a regular contributor to open mics, at such venues as DiVerse Gaithersburg Poetry and Roots Studio. She has been the featured poet at Words Out Loud at Glen Echo and participates in local poetry and prose writing workshops, in addition to reading, hiking, teaching, and enjoying time with her children. Her work has appeared in Beltway Quarterly, Mercurial Stories and Nightingale and Sparrow.

Ryan Quinn Flanagan is a Canadian-born author residing in Elliot Lake, Ontario, Canada with his wife and many bears that rifle through his garbage. His work can be found both in print and online in such places as: Evergreen Review, The New York Quarterly, Bourgeon, TheSongIs.., Cultural Weekly, Red Fez, and The Oklahoma Review.

Kate Horowitz is a science writer, poet, and essayist in Washington, D.C. Her work has been widely published, most recently in Unrequited: An Anthology of Love Poems about Inanimate Objects. You can find her online at www.thingswrittendown.com or on Twitter @delight_monger.

John Huey's student work of the 60's-70's was influenced by teachers in Vermont such as John Irving at Windham College and William Meredith at Bread Loaf. After many years he returned to writing poetry in 2011. Recently he has had poems presented in two issues of Poetry Quarterly and in the Temptation anthology published in London by Lost Tower Publications. Work has also appeared in Leannan Magazine, Sein und Werden, In Between Hangovers, and The Lost River Review. A poem regarding the Trump inauguration will appear shortly in an anthology to be published by Poets For Sanctuary (formerly known as Poets Against Trump). Perfume River Poetry Review will soon feature a piece in an upcoming issue regarding Vietnam. His first full length book, The Moscow Poetry File, was published by Finishing Line Press.

Donald Illich has published poetry in journals such as The Iowa Review, Nimrod, Passages North, and Sixth Finch. His chapbook, which will be published by Finishing Line Press, is "The Art of Dissolving." He lives in Rockville, Maryland. His blog is The Art of Dissolving.

Kelly Ann Jacobson is a Professor of English and the author of many published books, including the novel Cairo in White, the poetry collection I Have Conversations with You in My Dreams, and anthologies such as Unrequited: Love Poems about Inanimate Objects. She also writes young adult fantasy novels under her pen name, Annabelle Jay.

Luther Jett is a native of Montgomery County, Maryland whose poetry has been published in numerous journals, including The GW Review, ABRAXAS, Beltway, Innisfree, Potomac Review, Little Patuxent Review, and Main Street Rag. His work has also appeared in several anthologies, including "Secrets & Dreams, published by Kind of a Hurricane Press and "My Cruel Invention," published by Meerkat Press. His poetry performance piece, Flying to America, debuted at the 2009 Capital Fringe Festival in Washington D.C. His full-length manuscript of the same name was a runner-up in the 2018 Concrete Wolf Louis Award competition, and in the Washington Prize contest, sponsored by Word Works Press. His chapbook, "Not Quite: Poems Written in Search of My Father" was released by Finishing Line Press in the fall of 2015. A second chapbook, "Our Situation" was released by Prolific Press, (Summer, 2018).

John Johnson is a poet, playwright, native Washingtonian and the 2018 winner of the DC Project, an open-to-all poetry competition. Johnson is the founder of Verbal Gymnastics Theater Company and holds a B.A. in Theater from the University of the District of Columbia. He has received three artist fellowships from the DC Commission on the Arts, and other honors include participation in "Anacostia Unmapped," a radio project with American University's WAMU, in conjunction with the Association of Independent Radio, which captures the narrative of residents in rapidly changing communities.

Jacqueline Jules is the author of three chapbooks, Field Trip to the Museum (Finishing Line Press), Stronger Than Cleopatra (ELJ Publications), and Itzhak Perlman's Broken String (Winner, Helen Kay Chapbook Prize 2016). Her work has appeared in over 100 publications including Burgeon, Gargoyle, Beltway Poetry, Innisfree Poetry Journal, Little Patuxent Review, and The Broadkill Review. Visit her online at www.jacquelinejules. com where you will see that she is also the author of 40 books for young readers including the Zapato Power series and Never Say a Mean Word Again.

Holly Karapetkova's poetry, prose, and translations from the Bulgarian have appeared recently in Alaska Quarterly Review, Prairie Schooner, Drunken Boat, and many other places. Her second book, Towline, won the Vern Rutsala Poetry Contest and is available from Cloudbank Books. Find her online at karapetkova.com.

Sarah Katz's work appears in Deaf Lit Extravaganza, MiPOesias, RHINO, and The Rumpus. She earned an MFA in poetry from American University and has been awarded the 2015 District Lit Prize for Poetry for "The Beginning of Prayer" and a residency at Vermont Studio Center. Her poetry manuscript, Country of Glass, was named a finalist by former U.S. Poet Laureate Robert Pinsky for Tupelo Press's 2016 Dorset Prize. Sarah lives with her husband, Jonathan, in Fairfax, Virginia, where she works as the Publications Assistant at the Association of Writers & Writing Programs and is Poetry Editor of The Deaf Poets Society, a new online journal that features work by writers and artists with disabilities.

Charles David Kleymeyer graduated from Stanford University in Creative Writing, earned a doctorate in Sociology of International Development at the University of Wisconsin, worked in grassroots development in the Andes for 45 years, and is now a Senior Fellow at the Center for the Support of Native Lands. He is a Quaker pacifist, environmentalist, fiction/non-fiction writer, and performing storyteller. Kleymeyer has published five books, plus several dozen short stories and articles, and an award-winning historical spirit-quest novel about the New Testament saga (www.YeshuNovel.net). He lives in Arlington, Virginia, with his wife and daughter and has two adult offspring, as well. He has been writing haiku and exploring Buddhism for more than five decades.

Beth Konkoski is a writer and high school English teacher living in Northern Virginia with her husband and two children. Her work has been published in journals such as: The Potomac Review, Saranac Review, and Gargoyle. Her chapbook "Noticing the Splash" was published in 2010 by BoneWorld Press and a second chapbook, "Water Shedding," is forthcoming from Finishing Line Press.

Dwayne Lawson-Brown, aka the "Crochet Kingpin", is a DC native poet, activist, breakdancer, and fashion designer. He is one of the hosts of DC's longest running open mic series, Spit Dat DC, as well as poetry host captain for Busboys and Poets (450K location). In addition to featured readings at every Busboys and Poets location, SAGAfest Iceland 2015, Spirits and Lyrics NYC and Manassas, Woolly Mammoth Theater, and the C2EA "We Can End AIDS", Dwayne's short form poetry prowess led him to win the Best Haiku Award at the 2011 National Underground Spoken-Word Poetry Awards (NUSPA). His work to increase HIV awareness through spoken-word garnered recognition from the Congressional Black Caucus Foundation, BBCAmerica, the Discovery Channel, and The Washington Post. Ultimately, his goal is to force his audience to feel. He tends to meet goals. When not documenting his life through poetic meter, he can be found on the metro making scarves and hats, or singing karaoke.

Courtney LeBlanc is the author of the chapbooks All in the Family (Bottlecap Press) and The Violence Within (forthcoming, Flutter Press) and is an MFA candidate at Queens University of Charlotte. Her poetry is published or forthcoming in Public Pool, Rising Phoenix Review, The Legendary, Germ Magazine, Glass, Brain Mill Press, and others. She loves nail polish, wine, and tattoos. Read her blog at www.wordperv.com, follow her on twitter at @wordperv

Rebecca Leet has been widely published and quoted in newspapers, magazines, and books, during a Washington-based career in politics, policy and news. She turned her pen to poetry in 2015 after 40 years as a journalist and author. Her first poem was published in Passager in Winter 2017. She lives in Arlington and draws much of her inspiration from nature, whether in her backyard or idling along the Potomac.

Nick Leininger is a local DC poet originally from West Chester, Pennsylvania. Nick graduated from American University in 2017 with a Bachelor's degree in Public Relations and Strategic Communications. During his days as a student, Nick had his first poem published in the 2017 edition of Bleakhouse Publishing's Tacenda magazine. Today Nick works for a tech company as a customer success specialist. Nick hopes to grow as a writer and to continue his support of the arts. In his spare time, he enjoys exploring the various museums and art galleries of DC, engaging in physical activity, and continuing his quest for the perfect cold brew coffee.

Gregory Luce is the author of the chapbooks Signs of Small Grace (Pudding House Publications) and Drinking Weather (Finishing Line Press). His poems have appeared in numerous print and online journals, including Kansas Quarterly, Cimarron Review, Innisfree Poetry Review, If, Northern Virginia Review, Juke Jar, Praxilla, Buffalo Creek Review, and in the anthology Living in Storms (Eastern Washington University Press). He lives in Washington, D.C. where he works as Production Specialist for the National Geographic Society.

Lucinda Marshall is a writer, artist, and activist. Her recent poetry publications include Sediments, GFK, Indolent Books Transition Series, Stepping Stones Magazine, Columbia Journal, Poetica Magazine, and ISLE. Her poem, "The Lilies Were In Bloom" received an Honorable Mention in Waterline Writers' "Artists as Visionaries Climate Crisis Solutions".

Laura P. McCarty's creative work has appeared in The Rumpus, Lunch Ticket, descant, Jelly Bucket, the St. Petersburg Review, among other publications, including a family anthology of poetry My Mother, My Daughter, My Sister, My Self. She was a finalist for the 2020 D.C. Poet Project and a finalist for the 2016 Diana Woods Memorial Award in non-fiction. She earned a Bachelor of Journalism from the University of Texas, Austin, and her MFA from American University. Her debut book of poetry, Just One Swallow, was published in 2020 by Day Eight. Maryland Poet Laureate Grace Cavalieri described Just One Swallow, "A credit to the narrative tradition and has no superior. Her debut book is astonishing reading."

Mike McDermott has published poems in Minimus, Word-Wrights!, phoebe, Cabin Fever (Idaho), The Federal Poet, Frantic Egg 4, and Rustlings; a short story in Minimus; various non-fiction, and, long ago, freelanced about frolicking porcelain frogs for catalogs. He has an MFA from George Mason University and as president of the GMU Writer's Club organized readings for Margaret Atwood, W.D. Snodgrass, William Stafford, W.S. Merwin, and others. He has served on editorial boards of WordWrights! and GW Forum and is currently the Treasurer of The Word Works Inc. He has been an active participant in Washington, D.C, area poetry readings for several years.

Susan Meehan is the author of Talking to the Night (2017), and Goddesses Incognito (2018), and was the winner of the DC Poet Project in 2017, an open competition created to surface new poetic voices. Poetry is Susan's second, or third career. She recently completed a career in local government service, first as Mayor Marion Barry's constituent service director for Ward Two and subsequently as D.C.'s first Patient Advocate, providing services to the city's drug and alcohol addicts. Now retired, she remains active in local politics with her husband of more than fifty years.

Susan Bucci Mockler has had her poetry published in Poet Lore, The Cortland Review, The Paterson Literary Review, Voices in Italian Americana, and the anthology, My Cruel Invention, among others. Her chapbook, Noisy Souls, was published by Finishing Line Press. She is a poet in the Arlington County school system and teaches writing and literature at a local university. She lives in Arlington, Va.

John Monagle was born in Claymont, Delaware and raised in Las Cruces, New Mexico. A graduate of New Mexico State University, he is a resident of Rockville, Maryland and works at the Library of Congress. He has been twice selected as a Jenny McKean Moore fellow at The George Washington University and has been previously published in Minimus and Wordwrights poetry journals.

Annisha Montgomery is a recent graduate of Mount St. Mary's University in Emmitsburg, MD. Though she was first introduced to poetry and spoken word in the 8th grade, it was her time at the Mount that pushed her to write and share her poems with her professors and peers. She hopes to publish her own book someday.

Miles David Moore is founder and host of the IOTA Poetry Reading Series in Arlington, Va., and the author of three books of poetry. In April 2016, the Arlington Arts Council gave him an award for his services to poetry in Arlington County.

Yvette Neisser is the author of Grip, winner of the 2011 Gival Press Poetry Award. Her translations from Spanish include South Pole by María Teresa Ogliastri and Difficult Beauty: Selected Poems by Luis Alberto Ambroggio. Her poems, translations, essays, and reviews have appeared in such publications as Foreign Policy in Focus, Virginia Quarterly Review, Split This Rock's The Quarry, and the Bloomsbury Anthology of Contemporary Jewish American Poetry. She is a founding Board Member of the DC-Area Literary Translators Network (DC-ALT) and has taught writing at George Washington University and The Writer's Center. By day, she is a writer for an international development firm.

Neelam Patel is an Arlington, VA based writer, actress, and dancer. She's had the opportunity to perform as a featured poet at IOTA and Barnes and Noble. She feels fortunate to have acting credits including her solo show, Sari to Skin, and as lead in a traveling production called Interior Castle. She's currently finding public places around the world to stage short solo dance pieces.

Matthew Ratz is an author and performer living in Gaithersburg, MD. His poetry has appeared online in Bourgeon as well as on Huffington Post; his essays have appeared in Autism Spectrum News and The Atlantic. Matthew also performs regularly at La-Ti-Do, a musical theater and spoken word cabaret in DC. He is the author of several nonfiction books and most recently a chapbook, Lightning Bugs in Fragile Jars (2017). Professionally, Matthew is a mental health advocate and peer-support specialist with nonprofit organizations in the DC Metro area.

Jane Schapiro is the author of a volume of poetry, Tapping This Stone (Washington Writers' Publishing House, 1995) and the nonfiction book, Inside a Class Action: The Holocaust and the Swiss Banks (University of Wisconsin, 2003), selected for the Notable Trials Library. Her chapbook Mrs. Cave's House won the 2012 Sow's Ear Poetry Chapbook competition. Her essays and poems have appeared in publications such as the American Book Review, The American Scholar, Prairie Schooner, The Southern Review, The Sun, and Yankee among others.

J.D. Smith's fourth poetry collection, The Killing Tree, will be published in July by Finishing Line Press. His other books include the poetry collections Labor Day at Venice Beach (2012) and Settling for Beauty (2005), the humor collection Notes of a Tourist on Planet Earth (2013), the essay collection Dowsing and Science (2011) and the children's picture book The Best Mariachi in the World (2008). Awarded a Fellowship in Poetry from the National Endowment for the Arts in 2007, he has published poems in print and online publications in the United States and other English-speaking countries including The Awl, The Bark, Light, Nimrod, Tar River Poetry and Terrain. His reviews and essays have appeared in publications including American Book Review, Boulevard, Gastronomica, the Los Angeles Times and Pleiades, and his poetry and prose have appeared in several anthologies. Smith works as an editor and writer in Washington, DC, where he lives with his wife Paula Van Lare and their rescue animals. He tweets @Smitroverse and maintains the pages http://jdsmithwriter.com.

Mabel Ferragut Smith believes that poems are tendrils that coil between strangers, weaving secret, precise, intimate connections. She writes and reads in pursuit of that moment when the right poem meets the right reader, and magic happens. In addition to writing, she has worked as a choreographer and an architect. She lives in Maryland with her husband and two children, where she is the keeper of a Cuban heritage and beautiful dances, with a tiny forest in the background. She has poetry in Little Patuxent Review. Find her online at mabelferragutsmith.com or @MabelWrites.

Elnathan Starnes is a Wolf Trap teaching artist and local children's entertainer using the moniker, Groovy Nate (https://www.groovynate.com/). He was born in Wichita, Kansas, and attended High School in Denver, CO. After a 5 year enlistment in the Navy, he came to Washington, DC in 1989 and attended Howard University. From high school to present, he has been writing poetry that is now compiled in a collection of works entitled, Wichita Behavior in a DC Vibe - By Way of Denver (Oahu Visions).

Alina Stefanescu is the author of "Objects In Vases" (Anchor & Plume, 2016). She was born in Romania and lives in Alabama with her partner and four small mammals. Her flash fiction, "White Tennis Shoes", won the 2015 Ryan R. Gibbs Fiction Award. Her poem, "Oscar Dees, No Apologetics Please," from the chapbook Objects in Vases, was nominated for a Pushcart Prize. You can read her syllables in current issues of PoemMemoirStory, Tinge Magazine, Jellyfish Review, The Zodiac Review, Parcel, Change Seven, and others. More online at www.alinastefanescu.com.

Kate Stoltzfus is a writer and Midwest transplant living in Washington, D.C. Her work has appeared in Atticus Review, DCist, Education Week, the Chronicle of Higher Education, the National Catholic Reporter, the Journal of Feminist Studies in Religion, and elsewhere.

Rose Strode is a recipient of the "Undiscovered Voices" fellowship from The Writer's Center in Bethesda, Maryland. Her personal essays have appeared in The Gettysburg Review, The Little Patuxent Review, The Delmarva Review, and Viator; her poetry has appeared in Poet Lore. When she is not writing she wanders around in the woods looking for tracks. She enjoys gardening and fixing things that are broken.

Judy Swann is a poet, essayist, editor, translator, blogger, and bicycle commuter, whose work has been published in many venues both in print and online. Her book of letters, We Are All Well: The Letters of Nora Hall, appeared in 2014.

Marianne Szlyk is a professor of English and Reading at Montgomery College. She also edits The Song Is... a blog-zine for poetry and prose inspired by music (especially jazz). Her book, On the Other Side of the Window, is now available on Amazon. In July 2019, she was part of Tupelo Press' 30/30 Project. Her poems have also appeared in of/with, bird's thumb, Loch Raven Review, Solidago, Sycorax Review, Red Bird Chapbook's Weekly Read, Young Ravens Literary Review, Music of the Aztecs, and Resurrection of a Sunflower, an anthology of work responding to Vincent Van Gogh's art. She invites you to stop by her blog-zine and perhaps even submit some poems: http://thesongis.blogspot.com

Naomi Thiers' first book of poetry, Only The Raw Hands Are Heaven, won the Washington Writers Publishing House competition in 1992. Her other books are In Yolo County and She Was a Cathedral (Finishing Line Press). Her poetry, fiction, book reviews, articles, and interviews have been published in many journals, including Virginia Quarterly Review, Poet Lore, Colorado Review, Pacific Review, Potomac Review, Grist, Sojourners. She has been nominated for a Pushcart Prize and featured in anthologies. She works as an editor with Educational Leadership and lives in Arlington, Virginia.

Sally Toner is a High School English teacher who has lived in the Washington, D.C. area for over 20 years. Her poetry, fiction, and non-fiction have appeared in Gargoyle Magazine, The Delmarva Review, Watershed Review, and other publications.

She lives in Reston, Virginia with her husband and two daughters, where the recent demise of the household's fire bellied toad has officially raised her status to fourth funniest in the family.

Bernardine (Dine) Watson worked as a social policy writer for major foundations, nonprofits, and media organizations prior to taking a serious interest in poetry. She has written for The Washington Post, The Ford Foundation, Annie E. Casey Foundation and Stoneleigh Foundation. Dine's poetry has been published in the Beltway Poetry Quarterly, Indian River Review, by Darkhouse Books, and by the Painted Bride Art Center. She was a member of 2015-16 class of The DC Commission on the Arts and Humanities' the Poet in Progress Program, and the 2017 and 2018 classes of the Hurston Wright Foundation's Summer Writers Week. Dine serves on DC's Ward 4 Arts and Humanities Committee and on the selection committee for the Takoma Park Third Thursday poetry reading series. She's read her poetry in venues throughout the DC metropolitan area with More Than A Drum Percussion Ensemble. Dine is a current member of DC Women Writers of Color.

Kevin Wiggins is the 2019 winner of the DC Poet Project, an open-to-all poetry competition created by the non-profit Day Eight to surface extraordinary poets. Wiggins was born and raised in Baltimore, Maryland and performs as The Mysfit — a spoken word artist, storyteller, and playwright. His work stares adversity in the face and is unapologetic for the Black LGBTQ community with intensity, rage, compassion, and love. His debut collection of poetry, Port of Exit, was published by Day Eight in 2019. Amy Woolard wrote about Port of Exit, "These poems, and this poet, are a gospel."

Jessica Wilde is a D.C.-based writer of fiction and poetry. She grew up in a Navy family, moving frequently along the east coast of the U.S. and throughout Europe. She graduated from the George Washington University in 2008 with a degree in

English and Creative Writing, and received the Hassan Hussein prize for her thesis in fiction. She writes for the Works in Progress section of The American Scholar and is an Assistant Editor of Bourgeon.

Pamela Murray Winters has had work published in the Gettysburg Review, Gargoyle, Beltway Poetry, and numerous other publications. She received an MFA in poetry from Vermont College in Fine Arts in 2015 and is presently gainfully unemployed. A native of Takoma Park, Maryland, Pam lives by the Chesapeake Bay, hates seafood, and doesn't swim.

Katherine E. Young, poet and translator, is the author of Day of the Border Guards, 2014 Miller Williams Arkansas Poetry Prize finalist, and two chapbooks. Her poems have appeared in Prairie Schooner, The Iowa Review, Subtropics, and many others. Young is also the translator of Two Poems by Inna Kabysh; her translations of Russian and Russophone authors have won prizes in international competitions and been published widely in the U.S. and abroad; several have been made into short films. Young is a 2017 National Endowment for the Arts translation fellow and currently serves as the inaugural poet laureate for Arlington, Virginia.

Index

ABOUT DAY EIGHT

Day Eight's vision is to be part of the healing of the world through the arts, and our mission is to empower individuals and communities to participate in the arts through the production, publication, and promotion of creative projects.

Day Eight's programming includes an online magazine, poetry events, live arts programming, book publishing, arts journalism, and education programs for children and youth.

Example 2021 projects include:

The DC Arts Writing Fellowship was created to support early career arts writers. The project is conducted in partnership with local news outlets including Tagg Magazine and The DC Line. An annual conference brings together leaders in the field of arts journalism.

The DC Poet Project is a poetry reading series and open-to-all poetry competition that supports the professional practice of poetry. The 2020 instance of the DC Poet Project was produced through support from the Wells Fargo Community Foundation and the National Endowment for the Arts.

Day Eight's projects in local art history included an online archive dedicated to DC's first artist cooperative gallery, the Jefferson Place Gallery.

All of Day Eight's projects are made possible by the support of volunteers and individual donors, including the Board of Directors. To learn more about the organization please visit www.DayEight.org.

Day Eight